Peter Ellson – Detail from the painting by Emilie Gwynne-Jones—1969.
Reproduced by courtesy of Christopher Goode Esq.

Peter Ellson

Poems

Tuba Press
13 Bute Street
London

First published 1978
In a limited edition of 1,000 copies
By Tuba Press
13 Bute Street, London, S.W.7

ISBN 0 9505956 2 4 Hardback 500
ISBN 0 9505956 3 2 Paperback 500

Printed in Great Britain by
Latimer Trend & Company Ltd Plymouth

Contents

FRONTISPIECE:
Detail from the painting of Peter Ellson by Emilie Gwynne-Jones—1969—Oil 26½ in × 40 in. Reproduced by courtesy of CHRISTOPHER GOODE Esq and with the assistance of the artist.

Part I

Part II

Part III

Part IV

Part I

Gig-Saw

He found dividing ways—
Red roses for the living
Mind's eye that dissolves
Into the phantom of her presence:
And her heart the shroud.

Matter misting—Over turning
The prism's scale
In the deep sleep
Of the east wind;

On which the grey tormentor turns,
From the fated pairing
With her bone head bowed, mule head:
He the twain goth brute—Her anchor man.

The earth fatally sown
With the seed and the bone—
Risen in hopeless search
For a way round the inevitable.

The Origins of Excess

Aged—We all age—
In an impossible choice:
An objection to memory garbling,
Marveling, eye; that wreathes
The stricken—Guide mind.

Steeple sighted—Moulder
—Derailed—The iron divider,
Humourless annihilator.
Survivor—In stultified belief;
Stark charisma—Cloaking mind.

Free Tones of Bondage

Sovereign taste, tongued—
Between the young and boundless;
The swift deceiving
Wide eyed weary minstrels of phantasy—

The scales fallen from his eyes
Mirthless—Head in his hand—
The wind blown sheen sheer
Soft ark of the heart's holding, empty,

Gone out with the tide
Left in smithereens,
The shell fragments of dead memory
Spattering the damp sand—

Dear life; the bright loving
Soil of the human dream—
Soul of the wondering whole—
Sublime surrendering measure
Of whether, we are.

The Turn

In the turn taken—Past misery,
Icicle of broken desire—
Whisper on the wind waking,
Making into mind—
The bright horizon.

Gift taken
Swift the flowing memory
Weaving
A circle of stars;
And a crimson canopy that bears

Upon the bones of another life—
Fast found—Fragile;
The smile shrinks with the feeling
Woken within the other;
Neptune—Waving heavy over the water.

Ferry

A great ship—
The design of the world;
Cast off into the night

And the bell sounding out
A heavy tolling,
Through the sweep of the misting rain:

And I who am too sad—
In my vision and my memories
Forebode this not to be avoided journey;

The shadow of my life
Caught—Unprepared—
Accompanies me.

Heart

And my heart is heavy
With the hope of the departed;
My life poised in movement:

Dimension foreborne—In distraction—
—And every perception framed
By the delicately clinging veil

Of wind torn leaves—
Which yet the breeze
Cannot tear apart from the trees.

Again the advance of memory;
The division of the Soul:
Broken vision rendering

—And opening—In mystery;

The conditioning ends—
The function of suffering
Is absorbed.

The process of the mind,
To which I cling;
Is the territory of time suspended:

The concept of number assayed
Is a further projection within
The transfiguration of thought;

And each opens always again—

As that which is studied
Becomes sensible—
And is again divisible

For ever and ever:

So—Between two people
Who close together—
Through an ever varying landscape,

The climate in one short night
May decide the course of the river
For the next thousand years.

Toil

Constant action—
The chain of repeated acts:
The endlessness—Of production:
Each man making the one movement—
The one action—

Eight hours work
For a pound of flesh;
Virtue is in toil
For those who require it in others
Or like it for themselves:

Who do not see or care for the boundaries of life
That are crossed—
The ugliness and deprivation
Caused—In the lower depths.

Toil a bright thing on lucid terms;
Thine own terms, in the unhurried within
Span of the daylight journey,
Or the night's desire.

Toil—The natural tending Function;
The adjunct of survival,
Close by the life cycle—
The community's need and aid
That awakes with love.

Toil—That is spread across
The glow of the natural seasons;
That is the life of the land
Believing in that life proximity,

To death—On natural terms:
Child of nature—Gypsy of the Earth,
Based in the light of the sky
That passes within.

Overture

The overture is always playing—
The orchestra constantly renewed
In a forest of trees;
A flock of sheep—Grazing on the hill at dawn;
Highland cattle wading in the sea,
During a hot summer day:

A Pub in good heart;
An empty café in the early morning;
A paper shop on Sundays.
Low tide; the winter sea lapping gently:
My girl friend, naked, combing her hair.

Night-time and couples strolling slowly—
A man and dog in their familiar road;
The prams bearing slowly toward the shops:
Cleaning ladies invading Central London at dawn;
Children in their School Playground.

The roar of the home crowd, when their team trots
  into the stadium;
The evening street slowly filling with people at ease,
The restaurants opening gradually into night life;
A row of town houses peopled in the evening
And sounding with music and warmth.

Hierarchy

Torn
The needle sharp instructs,

Sing;
Love is beyond
Love beckons

Listen
Believe—
Rock upon my grave
I am here.
Begin.

I Am Seeing

I am seeing
The human dilapidations
Of poverty, illness and age:

Half a world—
One man's misfortune
Is the whole of another's life:

Uneasily weighing luck—Which,
Stretched by my imagination,
Almost encompasses the contradictions;

Deeply aware
That there cannot be
Only one possible road:

That out of the experience—Of the Spirit—
Through the sadness and the understanding
Has come an insight to appraise

And pass through
The boundaries of Pedestrian Logic—
To enter the dream acceptance

Of the act of being—
As the mind matter
In an identification

With the nature of transience
Becomes the vehicle
Of the limitless conscious.

Tetrahedron

The bright denial
And nerve-wracked riot
Of my mind—

Is the heartland
Of my ridden being:

Blind decision
Kisses the light
Of the Kite's keen hunger.

Single Arc of the Throw

Mind meeting misgiving
In the enactment of the possible;
The multiple reason round dimension
That is—The fail worn motion

Of the mind's river into anguish—Ridden.
Sight is the given gift;
See the heart—
Oh; the heart!
Weighing heavy in the scale;

And wrest out of this beckoning whirl,
The mind of the life essence—
Feeding wonder
To create light.

Fair son of silence,
The foreboding angel grows older—
The dice that are cast
Fall as partners
Upturned they become one.

Age

The almost stationary walk of an old, old-age
pensioner;
He passes, seen in the street through the open pub
door—
On a certain trajectory—Embodying the measure of
human prime;
A figure beyond oblivion's prolonged night of
gavotting;
Nurtured through the beginning, perpetuated
Past the limit of desire—The belief,
The divine given life, and a shadow.

City Funeral—
(For Pat Cutts)

Gathered—All particular and specific—
For the ritual of the dead.

Utterness to be muttered in finality—
Tryst—For the once only.

Confusion of flowers in the crematorium
Amid the unknown dead.

Oh—Spread your wings—

Shelter the one she is;
Cover her—Alone—

The drift of feather—
Sheaf of the woven heart.

Gathered—This moment,
For her—For ever.

Time

The truth understood too late: Time
For the whole man to measure again—
And weigh the wonder of the turning tide
That fronts our stark foreshore:

To heed the wind that gathers in the reeds,
And the risen sorrow
Over the clear gleaming damp of the sand
Echoing the ending alone on the Strand.

Knife Edge Blunted on Stone

Knife edge blunted on stone:
The kingdom—Weighing heavy—On bright lives;
Bones recall—We once were not.

I follow the course of the withered stream;
Stark void for the living;
Imago—I am the past: Now:
The wheel grinds.

The Fathers

It was then, never otherwise
Than understood,
Than unbelievably sad—

The sanguine memory is renewed,
Of a time that has passed away;

—The unknown men returned
To be gazed at by their children
And their neighbours' children

In an age of acceptance,
Nowhere—Without my memory—

Peopled by shadows
This land—

Lifeline

As I dog my own footsteps
I weep on the grass;
As I lift my pen
I feel the shadow.

As I become man mind,
I embody the birthright;
And take of my brother's life
In being as I am.

Loss

I wonder at this loss:
Bound to the earth—
I once walked sure
In body and heart:

Possessed willing strength
And a bright blazing fire in my heart
Where now the golden way
Lies cold in me.

Old Age

Thinking silence:
Silence working upon me.
Haven of your love-strewn dream
Answer that I own to—delicate hope—
My heart—I hold you dear—who range my wilderness

Kindled kith—green rift—blandished in craven
intricacy—
Human surety of child time;
I am old age—stationary—hold me,
I the old man on the bench in the King's Road:
Loaf of bread in a paper bag,
Looking past the passers-by.

Now the trees look well
And all is well
Bright dreams drifting away
In the wind's riff and love.

Adrift of the wind of winter;
Warning in the evening air:
I bearer of a stricken soul
Spirit of the blind, waning night
Now fall.

Billericay

The wavering heart—Flies
Down the long memory
Of the undone thing;
Our time the wished for woken wondered
Nostrum of delight, numbered—
As it was begun—For ever

Lovely as the blossoms—
And the green leaves
In the eye of my dream
Of the universal
Brave hours of youth.
Brain's child—Born of Cain—

Bluff—Brimming, hearty throated:
Lost on the broken coast;
Over the ever innocent earth
They trample and swing their clubs,
Bewhiskered and suited
Jovial brutes—'Cheeryho'.

Charisma—Unnerve me—
Across my hour the moment falls—
Out of blind eyes—
Hair of the head between
The need of man—Shorn.
In the dying flame

The desecration of the vital ember—
Iolanthe—Earth Child;
Flashing your temper.
Bewilder in the light—
Uncover your caverned wonder:
Your ungovernable love—

Sprite of the soil risen
Lilting above the level way:
Hope for the old man
Aglow; in your yellow eyes.

Part II

The Dream Bond

Humanity in the half glance—Aslant
The dream bond—
All are in pawn,
Redeemed out of the mind to die:
Which way to survive?

Oh, everyone has chance,
Before arms abandon
In the dark of the night—

The shades
Find heart in cool avenues,
Unfettered—But held together

Reaching back into nothing—
Yielding, through the wastes of legend
And iron-bound despair;
Their own Souls in pledge.

Ant Hill

Accolade of the Ant Hill
No one—As important as the many parts;
The multiple striving hearts:
Craving—Redolent—
Enshrined on a page.

Believing, grieving—Divested
Void of shell,
Many hours—Riven
In the slow ripple and flow

The bucolic rhyme out of mind:
Linking, far flung
Sight of the eye—Enshrining
The many enveloping fibres of being.

Desperate clutching at the possibility of pleasure—
Vision and possibility—Occlusion
Variation—Entry of the Blind Man—
Stark presence in the human temperament:

Dormant in the Dream. Shaken;
The shaven head
Ekes out atonement—In the lone life;
In the place without soul; identify the dead:

Through the touch of the Financier
Image of Croeseus—Voracious industry,
With the grasp of the Minotaur—Swallows
The cultivator beneath the autumn moon.

Distinct and holy veil between the stars—
Galleon of fate
Ocean—Isis—Thame—Running with the tide's
Relentless rending.

Origin

Separation—
The undertone within being:
Origin of the principal of two
Of reproduction
And wings.

Suffering—The mind seeks;
Tired on the time boundary:
Forsaken age remembering,
Slow in the spring
Strung easy—

Fifty years, condensed—
Look back—The dead past.
They speak of guilt so easily,
Who are not innocent.

In black and white
Sure and simple
They scratch at the underbelly of truth and verity—
Void in the centrality of their Being.

Measureless the moment
Of ending night,
After the dream murmuring and silence
Through the slow wondering arms of the dawn opening
Over the earth—Questioning—

The sea's creeping inevitable tide;
Final unfathomable mystery
Of the passing of our time.
The shutters of the night, closing
On the doomed self—

The scythe of the reaper—
Blind as the mystery of mind;
Phantom—In your kindness—Numbered
From the undercurrent's heave and swirl
Move out upon the endless plain.

Night

Grief: That is tomorrow;
Finite—Three throws finds faith:
Fidelity—And Resource.

Desperate and undone
In the Divine Dream
He could not wake,
Who woke the other,

Sleeping his swift deep saddening
Alone—In the wish-bone world—
Memory—How many dark fathoms down
To rest his head? To rest his head
Where the Park in the Night conceals.

Man Born To Be King

Born of woman—
Inspired by her,
Invigorated within her:
Victim of her power to create and destroy.
She is purpose and reason:
He is desire.

The world outside
Is ever using the user by stages;
The whole man waits to turn again—
To turn away—To turn away
To become a community—
In the form of the whole soul.

The Encounter

Surprise
In the moment of approach;
Element of mistrust after
The receding into distance
Shape;
Pre-occupied—Far away—
Turning about—Distracted;

Given to preservation,
Closed to; closing out:
He seems reasonable,
An unknown being
In the undertone of the ever eternal
Accosting stranger:

—Passed by,
Before the lever of contact
Triggers the psychical lock;
The hope in his being
Roving naked about the world.

The Trussed Spokesman

The trussed spokesman
Turning back
To precedent—Iron
Cold provider
Self salver—

Analysing:
Cheap and shoddy—But it pays:
Is it good?—Oh it pays—
We all pay—

Move in the wind of a feather,
Grope within the Soul's solitary rock
For the stark and solitary
Stump of all your philosophy.

Darkness

Confused in the warren—
Emotionally locked,
By the elemental mass.

Shape of being—
Deflected element of balance—
The figurine—Essential identification lost
In stupor of satiety.

The lone ageing man in the chair, bravely
Moving without hope—Through a Saturday afternoon;
Heavy and apart
The motion of his survival:
Heart driving on in desolation.

Night of the angel—Wild, wild,
Tearing of flesh, feeding
In her delicate way:

The night disappears;
And dawn's shades shimmering, rising,
Question oblivion.

Derelict

There is a certain
Desperate atmosphere in the air
This Friday afternoon—

Emptied out—
The Pubs' last customers
Are moving along—

Crumbling into the pavements
And padding down
The old basement step ways:

He appears out of nowhere:
In his eye—Compulsion:
Strained cognition—
He does not heed
Firm refusal;
But for a moment remains

Standing poised in my path—
Mind against mind;
Until—I order him
'Get on your way',
And off he darts lightly,
Vanishing like a phantom.

Nocturne

In anger
The beginning time over—
She silent—Sleeping
He—Wild awake: In the small hours
His garland out over the cradle creeping—

Back into the Earth—Mining his secret deeps
To the birth and the wonder
Of the whole heart's minding;
And the memory girl in tune
Shaking out her silken rhyme.

Oh a Reef;
A Barrier Reef
Between Beings—
In the dividing:

Fathomless the depth of desire
That ever surrounds
The hold of the heart
On the hanging head;

Understand—
He is half forsaken;
In the hope
He never forgets;

Neither gain nor loss
Nor the delicate spell of lasting reason
That breaks: As the heart
Which ceases to believe
Lays the lover to rest.

Your Calm Eye

Your calm eye surveying me—
My straying stream—Shed.
Demanded, I am denial
I suffer and you are my friend—
I live in tender, elusive quest of you.

Pole to pole—
Your lilac blossoming soul:
Shift of the shaping leaf,
Yellowing in the sun:
Heart's half-woken fertile dream
In drift of the gentle wind.

Mind

Mind binds the memory's wiles;
Separates the young who gambol;
Awakes the hopeless
To an image—
One with the least remembered:

While in a ceremony with the stars,
Birth is given to
The vision of two hands;
In the wake of origin;
And the form of function.

Conviction of belief—
In the blessing of knowledge
On the undertow of the current,
Thrown upon thought;
Blundering aghast in the nightmare.

Lying bound-hand and foot—
While hope the swain
Vainly moves mind
Within mind—And makes
Ending out of beginning.

Winchelsea

A surrounding dense sea mist
Breaks the line of the World:
A coldness envelops us;

The shadowy movements of cattle
Figure in the distance;

We are the forms and forces
Of human life.

Cooden Beach

The train to London passes Cooden Beach
And we are close in sight of the sea—
The waves breaking slowly and deliberately:
Rolling easily across the sand:

My long sad gaze turns from that Sea,
From this repetition of my childhood journeys,
And sounds out the distancing levels—
Reaches far inland—From Normans Bay
Into the horizon's mist;

And because I contain and recognize in myself
All the terrible cross purposes and causes
That make of sadness and tragedy,
I am without hope—For any of us—

Yet—What would I exchange for the heart?
Or my memory of the green fields' sway?

Hebrides

Mist, and the flame of beauty and hush—
The gentle empty road to the West
Rising and falling through the glens;
Under the looming, cloud-shrouded peaks
To the sea at Oban.

The boat winding past Mull, Tiree, Rum, Eigg
And on over the empty horizon
Toward the Outer Isles.

Stark grey—Wide waters battering the great Hull;
Broken white spray thrown spume—And the waves
Curling, crashing white, and boiling wind green—

A shoal of Basking Sharks rising round the boat;
And all the time dreaming through the present,
Over and over memory and distance;
Future turning back in the mind
And on, into an empty sea.

Aird An Runair—(North Uist)

Desolate far western shore—
Where the Atlantic lays on the white sand,
Breathes in the salt wind—
Wafting inland over the machair.

The great bay lying easy;
A slow sweep of whiteness meeting blue—
And the rambling ramparts of the Dunes
Standing in the stillness:
A concave line facing the distant waves.

The great bay slowly vanishes;
The heavy August evening mist
Carries in cold from the sea,
Across the sand
Over the Dunes and on

Shrouding the two lonely tents
Within its dense silence—
And floating slowly on
Spreading mystery
Over all this empty land.

Military Men

Steel gauntlet; mailed boot;
Overture of death and wonder:
Soldier of fortune
Bold in the eye's dance of glory—
Jaw riding the sun.

In all the deepest contradictions
Of extreme obedience versed;
Free of the bondage of the soil;
Yet twinned with death.

Kings are proud to place their garland
Upon the dead—
Survival—In the continuing
Of a high-hung aristocracy
The born martyrdom offering;
Burden accepting: Who lead, receive,
Defend, in hierarchy of birth,

And exclude the human problem
Which remains—In the contradictions
Of the growing older, forgetting,
Corrupted; quieted conscience:
Of life without love and without passion,
In the barren reflection of emptiness.

Image

Clinging flesh—
Wide tragic eyes
And the heart in sorrow

Before the utter
Being—
The ultra betrayal

Of the Soul
That was—
In the beginning benediction.

Life Given

Ever mingling, diffusing
The broad quarter shelves away;
Ripe gift of the rising heart;
Perception—Twists in the groove—
Rattles these bones
Drains this reservoir.

Conflicted into a gesture—
The moon glazed instant
Welded—Contused—Trembles
With the gilded life—
Extends the heart's half share—
Allows—Over and above,
That—Thou art.

The Green Dream

The green dream—That draws the townsman;
The world of the countryside and the sea;

The dream that gives a meaning to the life,
Which eventually falls through it:

To retire to the holiday places
Of one's childhood and prime;

To a beauty and atmosphere
A fragile reality

Not in itself susceptible
To be weighed or measured

But in the living void
Found wanting.

1916—The Mother

Alone—Close to the water—
She stood under the aspen trees;
In another land
Her eldest son was dead.

Dead—On this the third day of mourning—
She walked slowly—On familiar ground
Fifty yards downstream to the narrow footbridge,
Began to cross the weir—

Then she stood again awhile—Motionless—
Facing her passage—Looking into him—
Back into the face of her child,
Above the swirling Thames;

Then she fell—Swiftly, helplessly, endlessly—
And the silence took her body, and her life
Into the engulphing River;
The pulse of emptiness
Beneath a darkened sky;

Which for a long moment, held
Hovering over the water,
The shadow of her Soul;
Until she was gone.

Bone Hip

World without end;
People—A little longer
On the vanishing promenade;

In motion
And blessed rhythm
—Waking with hope—

The finite mind
A fusion of soul
And wonder

At rest—
In the first and the last
Saddening chimaera;

Turtle turning
Ever to an end that is beyond
The movements of the dance:

Carried by the heart's rebellion
Against the loss of the dream,
And the breaking by time,

Into the eye of the sailor, steady
On the point, which his ship must round:
World without beginning.

Part III

Nature

Man has only my bounty,
Given and taken, at will, my will,
Which knows only the demands of its dependents.

The seeds are long sown
Of my sad harvest;
Ever falling down
In all solitariness
With the lost life.

I am an immortal despot,
And you were conceived in bondage;
Defeat me you cannot,
Though you throw away your life in rage.

For all who are with me in living,
Come to me in dying,
And cease to be.

1960

The Living

Horror; all horror:
Enraged, we dwell outside
The encirclement of the spirit.

The dwarfing impossible, seen
Under shed hopes, emptied
From the arms of the dying.

Pierced and entered by a saddening,
The heart heedlessly bleeds
Upon each infinity of tragedy.

The shrine is within,
Torn, ragged, bloodstained
Trial of the dead.

1959

Destiny

Deep in man's being,
Concealed from eyes intent on seeing,
Perceive the faintly stirring fire
Of force over-reaching all desire.

Fateful few who feel the power,
Know your path is laid till the final hour,
After which, life's purpose done,
Greet the night, bid farewell to the sun.

Restless wanderer move on,
You mayn't linger, begone.
At sunset accept, and rest, and revive,
To wake at dawn, alive.

1958

Pale Hour of Dusk

Descending light down
On the green leaves lying,
Crisp leaves fallen:

Earth under me passing,
Unwound through the sky:
Heart broken on the breadth

Of silence; wavering
In the waking wonderment
Beyond the bright life.

Road

Severally forgotten—Undermined—
The striving die:
Untouched he threads his way;

Slowly pirouettes
With the great ungoverned,
Circles the spectre fed

The barren ones;
The walking dead
On their lonely road.

Wakening

The leafless trees wait in the hanging air,
And the unhurrying heron flies
Over the water of the river's passing.

There is gentleness born of the morning peace,
In the living light-loved world,
For thee, for thee, my love.

1968

Fields

Fields wreathed in the morning mist,
Mysterious, in the infinite
Defines of a phantom shroud:

Beauty upon the land;
Imagination dwelling in the silence
On the dark road through the fields.

Silence

Frail mist full fall of evening,
And the summer sad dying
Knowledge of autumn
In the leaves.

The river idling, widening
Wide beneath the white light sky,
And the high aspens, leaning, pale grey,
Cold upon their grieving beauty.

1968

Autumn End

After the first winter's night
With fog frost thick over the river,
The morning dawns in white-hung silence;

Leaves lie stiff on the ground
And trees, shrunk into the icy air,
Are alive with their stillness and the sky.

1967

Part IV

A Sequence of Eighteen Poems
(1972–3)
For Barbara Norman

I

Ah wraith of tender tears of soft despair;
We are breath before the light fades from our eyes
Into the darkness and the shadow's passing,
This the moment of the Soul, where two faces meet
And at last it is known if they are complete:

No more moments
To change places—Or acquire graces—
The twilight descends:
Leaving the world still turning.

II

A star-hung sky;
A hiss of water.
A roll of stones
A sweep of beach
A distant glow of headlamps against the sky;

The solitary lights of vessels on the horizon;
The Nuclear Power Station faintly glowing
Midst the dark water at Dungeness—

This morning you died
The silence is my love
And the sorrow of my heart;

The coldness is the touch of time,
Of mind awakening
I am here
With my belief
A lone hunter
Singing of the sea,
Sleeping with a folding of wings,

Creeping into your arms,
Grey light over your downs
Grey grief my eyes
Grey day seeking you
Grey home thine hair
Grey the quest,
In my greetings' meeting
My becoming with thee;
Now I am tender
And tremble to thee:
Cherish thee
Shell of a fragile thing
Out there on the water—

III

Look back from the other side of life;
Far away look in your eyes: From thither;
Malignly riven in body—On the last day.

I the remainer—The suspended being,
In the after life
My Brandy pocket, wandering
Immediate with grief:

In the Shadow,
With your dark flower
Held to my heart.

IV

Wide sky—Embracing
The great Square of the Churchyard,
And Winchelsea Church raised in the centre;

And chestnut-gold leaves hanging—Lying—
At the feet of the mourners—
The town's buildings in the peaceful distance
Surrounding the open grave.

The freshblown grass disturbed
And a spacious silence—Sounding
Goodbye—In the gathering making
—Burial of the Dead.

How close?
To awake to the drifting mirage which was:
The solid form of frail mortality;
Some season of the mind full meaning found—

Burden of beginning all over; once for all
—And turned—Twilight wise—About:
And out.

V

That certain line running through her every movement
Laying the life of her soul before the world;
I weaving a wreath of roses with my tears
And she so gravely loving: I arise
Remembering my Darling.

Deft innate essence, born to earthly shape;
Child out of the timeless distance of the unknown,
Ever aware, how imminent the return to origin,
On the other face of the Dawn;
To lay the tremor and tremble of her passing days.

I breathe the night empty of my dead girl,
Across the flat fields to the burial hill
Her arms speaking delicate certainty in their loving
  mime
To the high heaven's chosen memory;
Darling of the Red Rose.

VI

There was every reason to delight in her being:
Whence came that Soul?
She was the expression of thought; her care, shared,
To light and lift the hoping horizon of her friends;

Child so strong and rare; timid and daring;
In the shape of her reason—Ascending, evolving,
Meaning emergent, leading, the listener never
  overtaking:
Her heart's half glance would shape the heavens

And with a bright ribbon tie her gift;
While she reeled under her own instinctive doomed
  demand.
Shield her refrain—The way of her spirit—Risen
Into the sky—To hover and plummett—Dead in her fall.

VII

I am awake in her meaning:
Distant star—Dreaming deceiver;
Annihilation the mind's render
Riving

The sure and certain image;
Shaped in the grief of her
Fertile reason

Betrayal—Man genuflects,
In esteem configured:
Growing old:
Earth of ashen wonder—
Seeking.

VIII

In my travail
I awaken upon the cold earth
In the memory of her

Whose image overtakes every path I follow:
Lays me low—In despair,
Dogged by the deft delicacy of mind
The swift soft intricacy of movement;

Distant now—
The immediacy—
In the least response of her vital being.

IX

In that little space—She lived—
Cornered sanity,
Measured every moment—
Made thought paramount.

Scrutinised motive and personality—
Carved out a way for the heart:
Suffered the pain of care;
Cherished her demanding loved ones

The feline people.
Thought into my mind,
Kindled me—
I am memory—Committed—

She was twinned with death—
From the first Birth Gift
Under the edge of the Moon;

Now gone to earth
Bound—In the stream, floating
Accompanying, drifting—Untouchable—
Dream fast—In me.

X

Beautiful mind, nestling
Tender; the utter soul
Of the world, quieted by loss of you.
The age passing—That we are—
The time of our love—
And your existence—A preserve of memory,

That ever recurrent sense,
And immortal source, of hunger,
In the valediction of belief
Measured in lingering dream
And failing flesh:

From innate doubt,
Nowhere the slender vulnerability outdistanced,
Alone and yet not
You are beside me;

Sustaining
The shaping rhythm
Of the long breath of life
In the hope
Of my heart.

XI

I am
Thrust and thrown to the bone,
And truth the marrow;
Sorrow ever containing

Lifting the spirit
Holding harmony,
Venturing across the sand
Into dark waters; to die.

And the sure soft hope of the
Throat's plea to breathe
In the shadow of despair.

I awaken
To the eternal green hills
Falling into the sea;
The lost light in anguish

Only witheld
While the slow dream unfolds
Before my finding
Faltering steps.

XII

There is no way out—If the net is pulled tight;
Shrine of the beloved—All of us included—
Born shriven for the sacrificial triple throne threading
Interweaving frailty of shadow:
To leaven the passage of the life rite—

Beggared in death—
Raise the Crow's crested Soul
Armadillo—Endure—Stricken spirit—Found
Shaped of the inward distance.

XIII

Crossing into eternity
On an ebb tide
Blind hope of thee.

A wide space, flat dark between lights
Spreading, horizon reaching into night's
Mystery of unlit land.

Diameter of the infinite—Heart—My love
Pitch thy soul forward—Outstretched:
Strive in one glad sweep
To hold earth and sky together.

Human form,
Concentrated in precision of being:
Earth and the River that is night

Utter in the image,
In the soul's legend
Of the blood Rose.

Bare bones strike the earth;
End a life, an age
Of turmoil tragic turning,
Dividing ways.

XIV

The conflict of wish in restraint
Gentle water and darkness,
And the giving need;

Kindness the peace folding drift
And feral flower—
Ridden love;
Calm inimicable light;
Sighting, plighting troth.

Gaze—Through the distance and solitude
Memory regaining—Bright trailing—
Mystery—Across the marsh;
Searching out the mortal life.

XV

Thatch roofed a house
That burnt in the night away—
The heat is ended
In the motionless ash—

Fly with the eagle
Lifting leather wings—
In the spirit measuring
Distance powering feather.

Urge to survive the limiting world;
Decline of being,
No roof to our lives—
Adrift—Dragging anchors
In the surge and swell.

Mediocrity in the mind-spluttering void
Attempting an answer:
A thrust—
At limitless loss
That cannons off concatenation—
Draining the dross away.

Fixed in the fundament of decline,
Mind mediating—Body toiling—
Tempo dispersing the thought force
In annihilation. Give—
To bind beyond the grave,
And waken from the mind's demise.

XVI

At midnight, in the warm embrace—
Drawn drifting backward
To her bones
Cold on the dark hill:
In existence
The dead beckon;

And enter the sheltering life stream;
Dear heart awakened—
Joined across the distance—
With all that has gone before
Held—

Your hand offers
A longing—Resolution of grief
Formless with the birth of the child—And betrayal
In the dying—Beloved;
Shadow
Beyond advantage—
Shell of the night cracking;
Fallen into dust.

XVII

Now she lies dead in the first spring time;
Of her grave's ownership:
And will not be evicted,
Whose rented rooms were a Poet's loom,
Whose home for nine years was a wooden Barge,
Decaying on many waters.

She lies quietly in a Sussex Churchyard
On a hill in a sleepy town.
Shall I shelter her heart?
Shall she still shelter mine?
Shall the Salt wind raise her?
While I commit my grief—To the moon.
Who is it now—Which of us—That lives on?
One only is gone.

XVIII

The moon tide, turning mirror in flight
Of the ages innocent
In the abundant country garden:
The full foliage—at rest in the summer hour
Unseen, untried, never known to the autumn dead
In the quietude of the evening shore:
If ever exists.

Poems